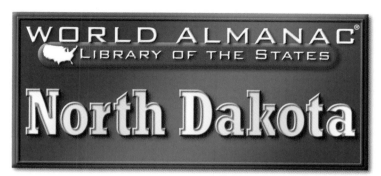

THE PEACE GARDEN STATE

by Justine Fontes and Ron Fontes

WORLD ALMANAC® LIBRARY

Please visit our web site at: **www.worldalmanaclibrary.com**
For a free color catalog describing World Almanac® Library's list of high-quality books
and multimedia programs, call 1-800-848-2928 (USA) or 1-800-387-3178 (Canada).
World Almanac® Library's fax: (414) 332-3567.

Library of Congress Cataloging-in-Publication Data

Korman, Justine.
    North Dakota, the Peace Garden State / by Justine and Ron Fontes.
      p. cm. — (World Almanac Library of the states)
    Includes bibliographical references and index.
    Summary: Illustrations and text present the history, geography, people, politics
and government, economy, and social life and customs of North Dakota, which
contains some of the Earth's most fertile farmland.
    ISBN 0-8368-5157-9 (lib. bdg.)
    ISBN 0-8368-5328-8 (softcover)
    1. North Dakota—Juvenile literature. [1. North Dakota.] I. Fontes, Ron. II. Title.
III. Series.
F636.3.K67   2003
978.4—dc21
                           2002041195

J
978.4
FON

Fontes, Justine.
    North Dakota, the Peace
    Garden State /

First published in 2003 by
World Almanac® Library
330 West Olive Street, Suite 100
Milwaukee, WI 53212 USA

Copyright © 2003 by World Almanac® Library.

A Creative Media Applications Production
Design: Alan Barnett, Inc.
Copy editor: Laurie Lieb
Fact checker: Joan Verniero
Photo researcher: Colin Scott
World Almanac® Library project editor: Tim Paulson
World Almanac® Library editors: Mary Dykstra, Gustav Gedatus, Jacqueline Laks Gorman,
  Lyman Lyons
World Almanac® Library art direction: Tammy Gruenewald
World Almanac® Library graphic designers: Scott M. Krall, Melissa Valuch,
  Katherine A. Goedheer

3 3187 00201 7370

Photo credits: pp. 4-5 © Layne Kennedy/CORBIS; p. 6 (top) © North Dakota Office of Tourism; p. 6 (center)
© State Historical Society of North Dakota SHSND SS-1; p. 6 (bottom) © Joe McDonald/CORBIS; p. 7 (top)
© State Historical Society of North Dakota Conserv 0739-v1-p11f; p. 7 (bottom) © Ed Wargin/CORBIS; p. 9
© Hulton Archive/Getty Images; p. 10 © Royalty-Free/CORBIS; p. 11 © State Historical Society of North Dakota
Conserv E0435; p. 12 © Colin Garratt; Milepost 92 _/CORBIS; p. 13 © CORBIS; p. 14 © State Historical Society of
North Dakota 0800-025; p. 15 © State Historical Society of North Dakota Tourism C2379; p. 17 © State Historical
Society of North Dakota 0075-224; p. 18 © Annie Griffiths Belt/CORBIS; p. 19 © AP/Wide World Photos; p. 20 (left)
© Terry W. Eggers/CORBIS; p. 20 (center, right) © AP/Wide World Photos; p. 21 (left, center) © Layne Kennedy/
CORBIS; p. 21 (right) © Farrell Grehen/CORBIS; p. 23 © W. Perry Conway/CORBIS; p. 26 © Richard Hamilton
Smith/CORBIS; p. 27 © AP/Wide World Photos; p. 29 © Joseph Sohm; ChromoSohm Inc./CORBIS; p. 31 (top)
© AP/Wide World Photos; p. 31 (bottom) © State Historical Society of North Dakota A1798; p. 32 © Joseph Sohm;
ChromoSohm Inc./CORBIS; p. 33 © Layne Kennedy/CORBIS; p. 34 © Richard A. Cooke/CORBIS; p. 35 © Farrell
Grehan/CORBIS; p. 36 © AP/Wide World Photos; p. 36 © Michael S. Yamashita/CORBIS; p. 37 (both) © AP/Wide
World Photos; p. 38 © State Historical Society of North Dakota Conserv 06-04; p. 39 (top & bottom left) © AP/Wide
World Photos; p. 39 (right) © State Historical Society of North Dakota 0262-03; p. 40 © AP/Wide World Photos;
pp. 42-43 © Hulton Archive/Getty Images; p. 44 (top) © Dave Bartruff/CORBIS; p. 44 (bottom) © Annie Griffiths
Belt/CORBIS; p. 45 (top) © Richard Hamilton Smith/CORBIS; p. 45 (bottom) © AP/Wide World Photos

Printed in the United States of America

2 3 4 5 6 7 8 9 07 06 05 04 03

North Dakota

Hardy Harvest

Journalist Eric Sevareid once observed that his home state of North Dakota is to most Americans "a large rectangular blank spot in the nation's mind." Yet North Dakota is full of fascinating places and surprising contrasts.

North Dakota contains some of Earth's most fertile farmland — and places that do not look like they belong on this planet! The interesting rock formations, petrified forests, and underground coal fires of the western Badlands seem like something from outer space.

Winters are bitterly cold and summers can be blazing hot. The state receives more than its share of ferocious weather, from hail to tornadoes. Yet, North Dakota enjoys a long growing season and supports an amazing variety of wildlife.

This extreme climate helps develop the resilience of the state's inhabitants, who pride themselves on finding ways to cope with nature's toughest challenges. Native Americans built ingenious shelters, as did early European settlers. Theodore Roosevelt credited his years as a Badlands rancher with shaping him into the man who would later become president.

North Dakotans express their lively spirit with celebrations. Every summer, the state hosts many ethnic festivals honoring the heritages of the various immigrants transplanted to its fertile soil. Music, dance, arts, crafts, food, and fun are the common elements in every celebration, even though the cultures are diverse. North Dakota grows more wheat than any other state except Kansas, and the state grows most of the country's durum wheat, the hard variety used to make spaghetti and noodles. Grand Forks throws an annual Pasta Party to celebrate the state's key crop.

Refugees from all corners of the world are discovering that North Dakota offers a chance to live in peace and solitude. If you put on ice skates and a smile, even the winters can be fun!

▶ Map of North Dakota showing the interstate highways, major cities, and waterways.

▼ The thousands of small lakes and ponds that dot the "prairie pothole region" of North Dakota make it one of the most important waterfowl breeding areas in the United States.

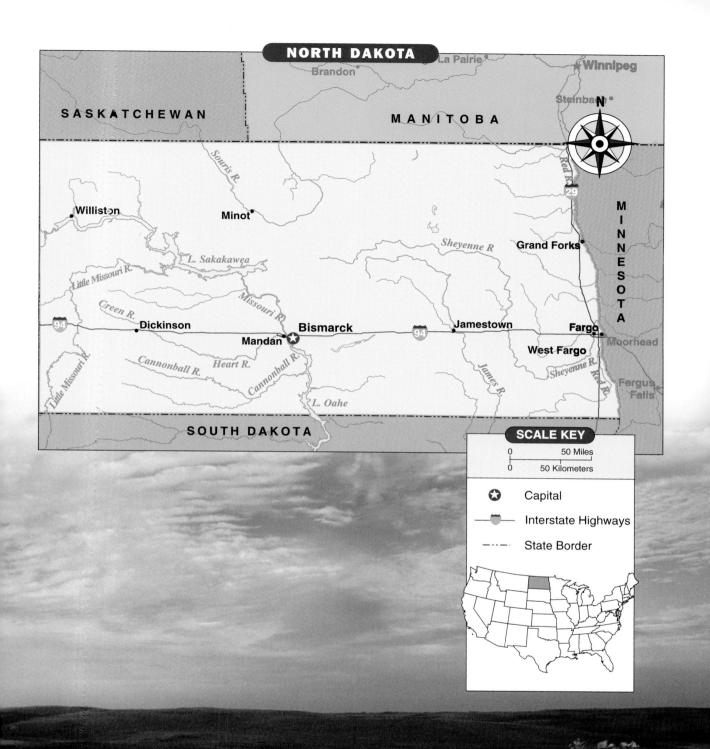

NORTH DAKOTA

SASKATCHEWAN

MANITOBA

Brandon

La Pairie

Winnipeg

Steinbach

N

MINNESOTA

Souris R.

Williston

Minot

Sheyenne R

Grand Forks

L. Sakakawea

Little Missouri R.

Missouri R.

Green R.

Dickinson

Bismarck

94

Jamestown

Fargo

Moorhead

Mandan

West Fargo

Cannonball R.

Heart R.

Cannonball R.

James R.

Sheyenne R.

Red R.

Fergus Falls

Little Missouri R.

L. Oahe

SOUTH DAKOTA

Fast Facts

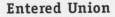

NORTH DAKOTA (ND), The Peace Garden State, Roughrider State, Flickertail State

Entered Union

November 2, 1889 (39th state)

Capital	Population
Bismarck	94,719

Total Population (2000)

642,200 (47th most populous state) — *Between 1990 and 2000, the state's population increased 0.5 percent. North Dakota's population reached its peak to date in the 1930s.*

Largest Cities	Population
Grand Forks	49,321
Bismarck	55,532
Fargo	90,599

Land Area

68,976 square miles (178,647 square kilometers) (17th largest state)

The town of Rugby is the geographical center of the North American continent. It is 1,500 miles (2,414 km) from the Atlantic, Pacific, and Arctic Oceans and the Gulf of Mexico.

State Motto

"Liberty and union, now and forever, one and inseparable."
— *Daniel Webster, lawyer, statesman, orator.*

State Song

"North Dakota Hymn," *words by James W. Foley; music* "The Austrian Hymn" *arranged by Dr. C. S. Putnam in 1926; adopted in 1947.*

State Bird

Western meadowlark

State Fish

Northern pike

State Flower

Wild prairie rose — *This hardy, bright pink flower is found in meadows, pastures, and roadsides throughout the state.*

State Grass

Western wheatgrass — *This tough, native prairie grass once covered most of the state. It provides grazing, hay, and habitat to many prairie animals.*

State Tree

American elm — *Often reaches heights of 120 feet (37 meters) or more!*

State Dance

Square dance

State Beverage

Milk

PLACES TO VISIT

Des Lacs National Wildlife Refuge, *Kenmare*
The lakes and wetlands along the Des Lacs River valley are a habitat for thousands of wild ducks, geese, grebes, and pelicans.

Five Nations Arts & Gift Shop, *Mandan*
See paintings, sculpture, jewelry, and baskets made by local Native American artists in a restored Great Northern Railroad depot.

Pfenning Wildlife Museum, *Beulah*
The outside of this amazing museum looks like a medieval castle. The inside is filled with stuffed exotic creatures from around the world.

The International Peace Garden, *Dunseith*
This 2,339-acre (947-ha) garden on the world's largest unfortified border celebrates peace between the U.S. and Canada with gorgeous flowers, as well as paths for hiking and biking. The garden hosts a summer international music camp, with Friday night concerts in June and July.

For other places and events, see p. 44.

BIGGEST, BEST, AND MOST

- North Dakota's State Route 46 contains the nation's longest curve-free highway. Cars can travel 110 miles (177 km) without turning their wheels once!

- The tallest structure in North America is the 2,063-foot (629-m) KTH1TV tower near Blanchard. Cables stretch from the tower far into the surrounding fields to keep it steady.

STATE FIRSTS

- **1934** The first international hole-in-one was scored at the golf course near Portal, where the tee for the 9th hole is in Canada and the cup is in the United States.

- **1933** A gas station owner near Casselton completed the world's first and only pyramid of empty oil cans. The 50-foot-high (15-m) pile of cans is still there.

Burning Beds

When coal catches fire, it can burn for many years. North Dakota's Badlands are filled with veins of lignite coal, a soft, brown coal that often ignites when struck by lightning. The lignite beds near Amidon have been burning slowly but steadily for over eighty years! At night, the fires can be seen for miles.

During his time in the Badlands, Theodore Roosevelt was amazed by the eerie look and sulfur smell of the underground coal fires. He wrote about the "lurid glow" and the "tongues of blue or cherry colored flame" that rose through cracks in the earth near the coal deposits.

Wacky Statues

The 46-foot-long (14-m) buffalo sculpture outside Jamestown's National Buffalo Museum is not the only giant animal in North Dakota. New Salem is home to the world's largest Holstein cow, a 38-foot-tall (11.6-m) sculpture made of steel and fiberglass. The city of Steele contains the world's largest sandhill crane. Harvey has a 20-foot-high (6-m) gorilla , a 44-foot (13.4-m) grasshopper, a 26-foot (8-m) walleye, and a gigantic turtle made from two thousand tires.

Amber Waves of Grain

> North Dakota is "one of the fairest portions of the globe . . . fertile, well-watered, and intersected by such a number of navigable streams."
> — *William Clark, of the famous Lewis and Clark Expedition, 1803–1806*

Native Americans of North Dakota

Arikara

Hidatsa

Mandan

Ojibwa

Sioux

The land that is now North Dakota was not always covered with waving wheat fields or even prairie. Thousands of years ago, the state was a thick forest full of great shaggy mammoths, mastodons, and bison.

Approximately 12,000 years ago, Paleo-Indians (prehistoric Native Americans) hunted these giant beasts. Gradually, forest gave way to grass, and a drier climate left the huge animals without their usual food sources. The Native groups were forced to leave the area to find other game to hunt.

Dirt Domes

About a thousand years ago, the Mandan people settled in North Dakota. They cultivated corn, beans, squash, and sunflowers. The Mandan built curved, wooden frames which they covered with mud to form big lodges in which they lived, protected from wind and weather. The Mandan fortified their villages against attack by warrior tribes. Before long, the Arikaras and Hidatsas joined the Mandan in the territory. These new groups also built dome shelters.

When horses were brought to the Americas by Spanish explorers, these Native groups became buffalo hunters. The Ojibwa and Sioux also hunted buffalo in North Dakota. Buffalo meat was a major part of the Native diet. Buffalo hides were used for clothing and building teepees or domed shelters. Buffalo bones became tools.

France Bows Out

In 1682, France claimed the region now called North Dakota. No Europeans explored it until 1738, however,

DID YOU KNOW?

North Dakota's coat of arms tells the state's history in symbols. The yellow and green represent golden grain and green grass. The arrowhead symbolizes the state's Native American heritage, and the crest signifies the mighty Sioux warriors. The fleur-de-lis represents Vérendrye, a French explorer. Three stars represent the three branches of government and stand for the coat of arms of Meriwether Lewis, of the Lewis and Clark Expedition.

when Pierre Gaultier de Varennes de la Vérendrye, a French fur trader, came south from Canada. After a brief look around a Mandan village not far from what is now Bismarck, Vérendrye returned to Canada.

In 1762, France gave its land west of the Mississippi to Spain. Thirty-eight years later, Spain returned the land to France. Then just three years later, in 1803, France sold the vast region called Louisiana to the United States in what would become known as the Louisiana Purchase. Half of North Dakota was a part of that deal.

Lewis and Clark Step In

In 1804 President Thomas Jefferson commissioned explorers Meriwether Lewis and William Clark to find a water route to the Pacific Ocean. The men were also asked to give a full report about the wildlife and Native people in the huge area the United States had just acquired. The two men headed a party of explorers who worked their way up the Missouri River. That fall, the party was in what is now North Dakota. The Expedition built a winter shelter near a Mandan village, close to present-day Stanton. They called the shelter Fort Mandan.

Sacagawea, a young Shoshone woman, met Lewis and Clark that winter. Sacagawea, her husband, and her infant son joined the Expedition when it resumed in the spring.

▼ A reconstructed Mandan lodge shows how North Dakota's early inhabitants built their homes from materials available on the prairie.

Sacagawea taught the explorers how to find edible plants. Acting as guide and interpreter, she helped them pass safely through Shoshone territory. Despite getting sick several times, Sacagawea completed the yearlong journey to Oregon.

Settlers, Sioux, and Soddies

In 1812, North Dakota received its first permanent white settlement. Braving the rough climate and isolation, a group of Scottish and Irish farmers from Canada built rough log cabins to create a trading post in Pembina. In 1818, Great Britain agreed to let the United States own the half of North Dakota not covered by the Louisiana Purchase. Preferring to stay under British rule, most of the Pembina settlers moved back to Canada. Many of those who remained married Native American women.

Congress created the Dakota Territory in 1861. The territory included much of modern-day Montana and Wyoming, as well as North and South Dakota. The population of the territory was slow to grow because of poor transportation and fear of attack from Native tribes. In 1862, Sioux warriors killed hundreds of settlers in Minnesota. Some of the warriors fled to the Dakota Territory. The federal government sent troops into the territory to punish the warriors who had taken part. Several fierce battles were fought as the troops pursued the Sioux across the Dakota Territory.

▼ Route map of the Northern Pacific Railroad circa 1871. Construction of the railroad, which traveled through the Dakota Territory across the United States, began in 1870 and was finally completed in 1883.

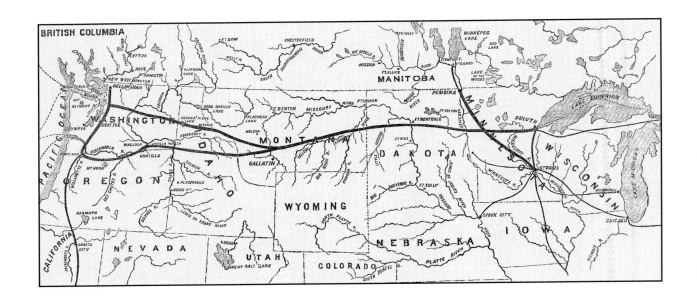

The U.S. government signed several treaties with the tribes in the Dakota Territory, granting them land on reservations. The government often broke the treaties, which caused more unrest.

In 1863, President Abraham Lincoln passed the Homestead Act to encourage more settlement in the Dakota Territory. The law offered 160 acres (65 hectares) of free land to anyone who lived on a claim for five years.

To keep their claims under the Homestead Act, settlers had to build a claim shack 12 by 14 feet (3.7 by 4.3 m) or larger. But how could settlers build when the land was just an endless sea of wild grass, with very few trees? And how could they farm until they broke the sod (the thick layer of grass and soil) covering the prairie? Resourceful settlers discovered that solving one problem solved the other. They built homes by stacking thick chunks of sod like bricks. With walls and roofs 3 feet (0.9 m) thick, the resulting "soddies" were warm in the winter and cool in the summer. The only problems were earth-loving bugs and leaks during heavy rains.

The settlers also learned to use the prairie's constant wind. They built windmills to pump water from underground to the earth's surface. Windmills are still used today on many farms in western North Dakota.

Many settlers were overwhelmed by the climate's extremes of heat, drought, wind, cold, giant hail, as well as prairie fires started by lightning. Grasshopper swarms could devour entire fields of crops in a day! For many pioneers, the prairie's isolation was the toughest challenge: Settlers could literally go for miles without seeing another person.

And Then Came the Railroad

When the Northern Pacific laid tracks as far as Fargo by 1872, North Dakota's two biggest problems, communication and transportation, were beginning to end. Finally, there was an easy

William Clark

Lewis and Clark met in the army when they served in the Indian campaign of 1793. At twenty-three, Clark had started to develop his skills as a frontiersman and naturalist. Clark and Lewis lost touch for several years. Then, in 1803, President Thomas Jefferson asked Lewis to lead the first U.S. expedition to explore the territory between the Mississippi River and the Pacific Ocean. (Lewis and Jefferson had been childhood neighbors.) Lewis asked his old army friend, Clark, to be coleader of the Expedition. Despite their past frontier experience with Native Americans, Lewis and Clark gladly accepted the help of a young Shoshone woman they met in North Dakota. Sacagawea contributed greatly to the success of their difficult journey.

William Clark's friendship with Native Americans continued. Upon his return to Washington in 1807, Clark was appointed superintendent of Indian affairs, a post he held for thirty years. The job gave Clark a chance to shape the government's policy toward the West.

way to move people and goods over the prairie. Towns with newspapers, stores, and banks sprang up along the tracks.

Immigrants seeking free, fertile, land poured in from Norway, Germany, Russia, Sweden, and other countries. Settlers from the eastern United States also moved west. Between 1890 and 1910, North Dakota's population more than doubled.

Statehood

During the 1870s, settlers started asking Congress to divide the Dakota Territory into two parts. Population centers had developed in the northeast and the southeast. North-south travel between these centers was hard, because the railroads laid their tracks from east to west. With little in common, the two groups of settlers wanted their own governments.

▼ The railroad did much to solve North Dakota's biggest problems: communication and transportation. Large freight engines, such as this one, sometimes pulled mile-long freight trains across the Plains.

The word *Dakota* means "friends" or "allies." It is what the Sioux called themselves. In February 1889, Congress established the boundary between North and South Dakota. On November 2, 1889, North Dakota became the thirty-ninth state and South Dakota the fortieth.

Bonanza to Bust

With the railroad came huge wheat farms in the fertile Red River Valley. Eastern corporations and a few wealthy families founded farms as large as 65,000 acres (26,305 ha). Thanks to the fertile soil, modern machinery, and orderly methods of planting, harvesting, and marketing a single crop (wheat), these giant farms made giant profits. In fact, they were so successful they became known as "bonanza farms." When word of their profits spread, thousands of settlers rushed to North Dakota.

At the same time, cattle companies from the southern plains moved into the Badlands. Theodore Roosevelt, the future president, was one of the ranchers who opened up the land along the Little Missouri River.

Many farmers, however, went broke when wheat prices crashed in 1890. Cattle ranchers in the western part of the state discovered that the Badlands were aptly named. Many herds died of thirst in the blistering summer heat or froze in winter's icy grip. The majority of North Dakota's settlers didn't make it through the five years required by the Homestead Act.

Farmers who stayed wound up in debt. Banks, grain companies, and railroads charged farmers high interest rates and fees. The farmers also did not like how much power out-of-state businesses had over North Dakota politics. In 1915, fed-up farmers formed the Nonpartisan League in order to create state-owned banks, which would give farmers low-interest loans, and state-owned flour mills, grain elevators, packing houses, and cold-storage plants with lower fees for processing and storing grain. The Bank of North Dakota and the North Dakota Mill and Elevator still serve the state's farmers. Thousands of North Dakota farmers joined the league. Soon, League candidates won almost all state offices. They gave farmers tax breaks and increased funding for local schools.

▲ Steamboats like the *Rosebud* in this 1878 photograph brought troops, freight, mail, and passengers to settlements along the Missouri River. As business grew, steamboats often connected with railroads to transport goods and people.

DID YOU KNOW?

Special trains brought professional hunters west to shoot buffalo. The hunters shot through the windows, leaving the dead animals to rot on the Plains. One man could kill hundreds in a day. By 1889, only 541 buffalo were left in the whole country. The tribes who depended on them for meat, clothes, and shelter were devastated and confined to one of North Dakota's four Indian reservations.

In the 1920s, once again, wheat prices tumbled. When the banks failed, most people lost their meager savings, and many farmers were financially ruined.

Depression, Drought, and Recovery

In 1929, the U.S. stock market crashed, plunging the entire nation into the Great Depression. North Dakota was hit especially hard, because in the early 1930s, the state was also struck by a terrible drought. Huge clouds of dust carried off the topsoil. The dust was so thick that people had to turn on lights during the day just to see inside their homes!

The worst year of the drought was 1936. The wheat harvest was a disaster in almost every county of the state. Between 1932 and 1937, the income per person in North Dakota was just 47 percent of the national average. By 1939, most North Dakota farmers had lost their land and many had fled the state.

Government construction projects helped put North Dakotans back on their feet. Unemployed people built highways, bridges, and buildings, many of which are still used today. The State Water Conservation Commission was also created to help farmers irrigate their land and prevent soil erosion. Since then, state, federal, and private agencies have established various projects to encourage "dry farming," methods that make the most of North Dakota's limited rainfall.

The drought was over by the time the United States joined World War II. North Dakota wheat harvests were eagerly purchased by the U.S. armed forces. Unfortunately, by the end of the 1940s, wheat prices dropped again because of farm surpluses throughout the country. The increased use of machinery left large numbers of farmworkers unemployed. Many North Dakotans left the countryside to seek jobs in the cities or out of state.

RIVERDALE
SPILLWAY
MISSOURI RIVER
EMBANKMENT
MISSOURI RIVER
SWITCHYARD
OUTLET CHANNEL
POWERHOUSE
INTAKE STRUCTURE

GARRISON DAM AND RESERVOIR

Photo Date June 1953

▲ The Garrison Dam took seven years to build. It transformed the Missouri River drainage and ecosystems in central North Dakota and created both economic and recreational opportunities for the state's citizens.

DID YOU KNOW?

The Garrison Dam took 9 million truckloads of dirt and 1,500,000 cubic yards (1,153,846 cubic meters) of concrete to build. It also took seven years and $300 million. It is the fifth-largest earthen dam in the United States. In an average year, it generates 2,600,000 megawatt hours of electricity.

Since World War II, North Dakota's economy has improved. In 1947, construction began on the great Garrison Dam. The dam helps control flooding, creates hydroelectric power, and provides water for irrigation. It also created Lake Sakakawea, one of the world's largest artificially created lakes and a favorite spot for fishing, boating, and recreation.

In 1951, oil was discovered near Tioga. Some people found jobs in the oil industry, although this was not a complete solution to the state's economic struggles. In 1957, North Dakota established an Economic Development Commission to attract industry to the state. More than eighty communities created their own commissions, which boosted the state's industrial growth to the highest in the country between 1958 and 1969.

No News Is Good News

While industry has been slow to grow in North Dakota in recent history, tourism is on the rise. When popular tourist destinations in other states are suffering from overcrowding and pollution, North Dakota can boast clean lakes and rivers crowded with fish, not people. The state now has five tribal casinos that are beginning to attract both tourists and conventions.

Governor John Hoeven, in his 2002 State of the State address, said that North Dakota is building its future on six pillars: education, economic development, agriculture, energy, technology, and quality of life. North Dakota does not often come up in the news. Life in the state is peaceful, and North Dakotans are happy to keep it that way.

Preserving the Past

North Dakota's future rests on its past. The state's history has shaped its occupants, their attitudes, and their ways of doing things. Now it is the foundation for the state's vital tourist industry. Visitors come to see a place where fields still dominate the landscape, small towns are still friendly, and there are more fish than people who fish. North Dakota offers a chance to fish year-round in a variety of settings, including lakes, rivers, waterfalls, and through the ice. Since fish populations are so healthy, many fish are caught in unlimited quantities, including bluegill, crappie, white bass, and rock bass. The limit for salmon is five fish per day.

Below: Lake Sakakawea is just one of the many places for boating, fishing, and other outdoor activities in North Dakota. The lake draws sports enthusiasts from many parts of the country and contributes to the state's growing tourist industry.

Yearning to Breathe Free

> 40-below keeps out the riffraf.
> —*A popular North Dakota expression*

For a state with the fourth-lowest population in the union, North Dakota has a surprising amount of diversity. After the Homestead Act of 1863 offered free land to settlers and the bonanza farms of the 1870s dangled the possibility of huge profits, people flocked to the state. Settlers came from the east and the south, as well as from Europe and Canada. By 1910, over 70 percent of North Dakota's residents were either immigrants or the children of immigrants. This was the highest percentage of foreign-born residents in the nation at that time.

Settlers from Norway and other Scandinavian countries were among the first to farm and build on North Dakota soil. Many others followed. Norwegians settled throughout the state. Germans and Russians concentrated in the south-central area. Canadians moved into the northern Red River Valley.

Age distribution in North Dakota
(2000 Census)

0–4	39,400
6–19	144,064
20–24	50,503
25–44	174,891
45–64	138,864
65 & Over	94,478

Across One Hundred Years
North Dakota's three largest foreign-born groups for 1890 and 1990

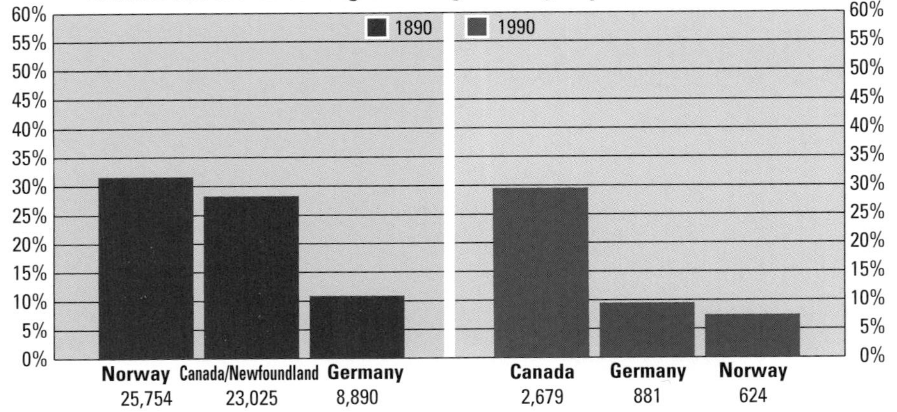

1890
- Norway: 25,754
- Canada/Newfoundland: 23,025
- Germany: 8,890

Total state population: 182,719
Total foreign-born: 81,461 (44.6%)

1990
- Canada: 2,679
- Germany: 881
- Norway: 624

Total state population: 638,000
Total foreign-born: 9,388 (1.5%)

Patterns of Immigration

The total number of people who immigrated to North Dakota in 1998 was 472. Of that number, the largest immigrant groups were from Canada (18%), India (8.7%), and Cuba (3.8%).

The largest groups of immigrants came to North Dakota from Norway, Germany, England, and Ireland. Armenians, Bulgarians, Finns, Greeks, Poles, Swedes, and other ethnic groups also founded communities in North Dakota. Near Minot, Lebanese Muslims built a mosque. The prairie beyond Bismarck and Devils Lake was settled by Russian Jews. Although North Dakota is home to people from many different faiths, over half the religious congregation members in the state belong to either the Roman Catholic or Lutheran Church.

▲ Folk festivals were popular in North Dakota as far back as 1900.

From Far Away to Fargo

Recently, Mexican migrant workers, who used to come to North Dakota in the summer to pick fruits and vegetables, have chosen to stay year-round. Chinese, Indians, Filipinos, and Vietnamese have also discovered North Dakota as a place to settle. Fargo is now home to refugees from troubled places all over the world. People fleeing wars and other undesirable living situations in Bosnia, Cambodia, Haiti, Iraq, the Sudan, and Zaire find North Dakota's largest city a peaceful haven.

DID YOU KNOW?

One of the biggest gatherings of Native Americans in the United States is the United Tribes International Powwow. In Sioux tradition, a powwow is more than a great celebration full of friendship, food, and music; it is a prayer to Wakan-Tanka, the Great Spirit or Grandfather.

Heritage and Background, North Dakota   Year 2000

▶ Here is a look at the racial back-grounds of North Dakotans today. North Dakota ranks forty-sixth among all U.S. states with regard to African Americans as a percentage of the population.

Note: 1.2% (7,786) of the population identify themselves as **Hispanic** or **Latino,** a cultural designation that crosses racial lines. Hispanics and Latinos are counted in this category as well as the racial category of their choice.

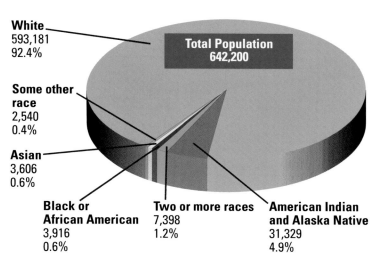

White 593,181 92.4%

Total Population 642,200

Some other race 2,540 0.4%

Asian 3,606 0.6%

Native Hawaiian and Other Pacific Islander 230 0.0%

Black or African American 3,916 0.6%

Two or more races 7,398 1.2%

American Indian and Alaska Native 31,329 4.9%

Despite these new arrivals, the big boom in North Dakota's immigration was between 1870 and 1910. Today, about 95 percent of North Dakotans were born in the United States. Most are of German and Norwegian descent.

Native Americans

Various tribal traditions contribute to North Dakota's Native American heritage. Though each Native group has its own particular history and customs, most share a deep respect for Earth. Annual gatherings give North Dakota's young Native Americans a chance to learn tribal dances and crafts and to help keep their ancestral traditions alive. Museums display artifacts left by the state's ancient inhabitants, as well as the arts and crafts of today's Native Americans.

North Dakota has five Indians reservations: Fort Totten, Fort Berthold, Turtle Mountain, Standing Rock, and Sisseton.

Educational Levels of North Dakota Workers (age 25 and over)	
Less than 9th grade	35,658
9th to 12th grade, no diploma	30,298
High school graduate, including equivalency	113,931
Some college, no degree or associate degree	138,855
Bachelor's degree	67,551
Graduate or professional degree	22,292

▼ Aerial skyline view of downtown Fargo, North Dakota's largest city.

Small Cities

Even North Dakota's biggest cities are small. Only seventeen of North Dakota's cities have more than twenty-five hundred people. Only four have more than twenty-five thousand! From largest to smallest these are Fargo, Grand Forks, Bismarck, and Minot. About one-third of the state's residents live in these four cities. Only about half of North Dakota's residents live in urban areas. Reflecting the state's agricultural heritage, many North Dakotans still enjoy rural or small-town life.

Fargo, North Dakota's largest city, has only about 90,599 people. Many young people are eager to move to cities with more excitement and a wider variety of foods, stores, art, and activities. But others appreciate the lack of traffic, the clean air, and the friendly pace.

How Ya Doin'?

Walk the streets of North Dakota and you will hear this phrase often. The residents are known for being both friendly and helpful.

The state boasts one of the lowest crime rates in the country. North Dakotans generally do not bother to lock their houses or cars. In winter, when cars are hard to start, drivers often leave their engines running while they go shopping or have dinner.

Education

North Dakota's first school was established by Roman Catholic missionaries at Pembina in 1818. The school closed in 1823 when Pembina was abandoned. In the state's early days, teachers traveled from village to village, teaching groups of children in homes. As towns grew, the settlers built schools, with materials supplied by the railroads, which were eager to attract more settlers.

In 1862, the first legislature of the Dakota Territory voted for the creation of public schools. North Dakota now has 276 public school districts, 61 nonpublic schools, and 7 Bureau of Indian Affairs schools. Children are required to attend school from age seven to sixteen. The state's first institution of higher learning, the University of North Dakota, opened its doors in 1883. Others followed soon after.

▲ Two thousand North Dakotans set a new record for snow angels in an attempt to get into the *Guinness Book of World Records*.

Tribal Names

The names of North Dakota's Indian tribes have special meaings. The Mandan call themselves "the People of the First Man" and believe their presence in North America dates from the beginning of time.

The Hidatsa were known as the Minnetaree or Gros Ventre. Minnetaree means "to cross the water." The names Arikara, Ricarees, and Rees were given by the Pawnee to describe the way the Arikaras wore their hair — tied with two upright bones.

Fierce, Flat, and Fertile

> The wind in North Dakota is an almost living presence. At the height of a prairie gale, it can blow a straw through a 2-inch [5-centimeter] plank, propel snow through the tightest seam at window or door, and send dust through any man-made barrier.
>
> — *North Dakota: A Bicentennial History by Robert P. Wilkins and Wynona Huchette Wilkins, 1977*

North Dakota is one of the coldest, hottest, and windiest places in the United States. With few trees to slow it down, the wind picks up speed as it crosses the Plains, carrying dust, snow, and whatever else is in its path.

In some parts of North Dakota, winter temperatures do not rise above freezing for months on end. Temperatures below 0 degrees Fahrenheit (-18 degrees Celsius) are common. Droughts are a constant threat. Floods, tornadoes, and hailstorms can also wreak havoc.

North Dakota's harsh winters and hot summers are typical of a "continental climate." This climate occurs wherever a large land mass does not have the weather-easing benefits of a big body of water nearby. North Dakota, at the center of the North American continent, is bordered by Montana on the west, South Dakota on the south, Minnesota on the east, and the Canadian provinces of Manitoba and Saskatchewan on the north.

Highest Point

White Butte
3,506 feet (1,069 m) above sea level

▼ *From left to right:* a red fox hunts during winter; a tornado sweeps through the prairie; a blizzard makes travel difficult; ducks enjoy the marsh in the prairie pothole region; rock formations typical of the badlands; a cowboy rounds up wild horses.

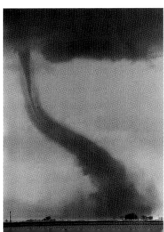

Three Major Divisions

North Dakota's 70,700 square miles (183,112 sq km) are divided into three parts: the Red River Valley, the Rolling Drift Prairie, and the Great Plains.

The Red River Valley is an extremely flat strip of some of the world's best farmland. It supports dairy farms and bumper crops of a variety of grains, including wheat.

The Rolling Drift Prairie rises gradually west and southwest of the Red River Valley. Giant masses of ice called glaciers moved across this region during the Ice Age. As they moved, the glaciers left behind rich deposits of earth called "drift." This area is dotted with thousands of low hills. Between the hills are lakes and ponds that look like big potholes — hence its nickname, "prairie pothole region." Some lakes appear when the snow melts in the spring. Many are gone by summer's end. When they are full, the lakes play host to a huge variety of breeding birds. Only Alaska breeds more waterfowl than North Dakota.

The southwestern half of North Dakota is part of a huge highland, the Great Plains, that stretches from northern Canada to southern Texas. A narrow band of lowlands called the Missouri Breaks follows the Missouri River. This hilly area makes good grazing land for cattle and is rich in mineral deposits. It contains many buttes (steep hills that stand alone).

Also in the southwest are the Badlands, a sandstone, shale, and clay valley carved into unique formations by wind and water. The Badlands got their name from French traders who found the steep, broken hills "bad-for-traveling."

Lakes and Rivers

Many streams, rivers, lakes, and springs make up North Dakota's water resources. Devils Lake is the largest natural

Average January temperature
Bismarck: 8°F (−13.3°C)
Fargo: 5.5°F (−14.7°C)

Average July temperature
Bismarck: 70.5°F (21.4°C)
Fargo: 71°F (21.7°C)

Average yearly rainfall
Bismarck: 16 inches (40.6 cm)
Fargo: 20 inches (50.8 cm)

Average yearly snowfall
Bismarck: 38 inches (96.5 cm)
Fargo: 35 inches (88.9 cm)

Largest Lakes
Lake Sakakawea 368,000 acres (148,924 hectares)
Devils Lake 100,000 acres (40,469 ha)
Lake Oahe 31,400 acres (12,707 ha)

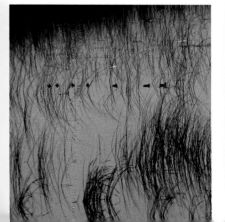

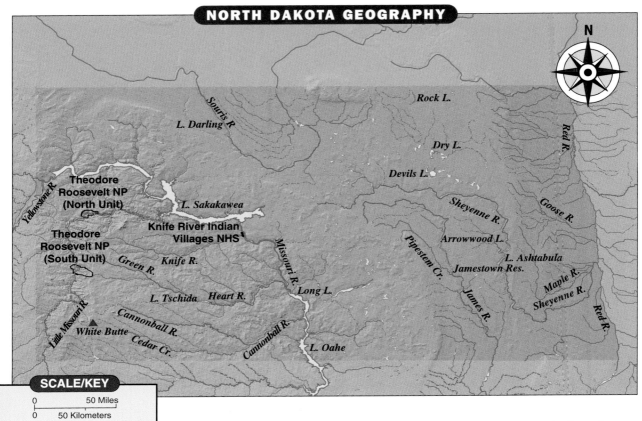

NORTH DAKOTA GEOGRAPHY

N

Souris R.
L. Darling
Rock L.
Dry L.
Devils L.
Red R.
Yellowstone R.
Theodore
Roosevelt NP
(North Unit)
L. Sakakawea
Sheyenne R.
Goose R.
Theodore
Roosevelt NP
(South Unit)
Knife River Indian
Villages NHS
Arrowwood L.
L. Ashtabula
Jamestown Res.
Green R.
Knife R.
Missouri R.
Pipestem Cr.
Maple R.
Little Missouri R.
L. Tschida
Heart R.
Long L.
Sheyenne R.
Cannonball R.
James R.
White Butte
Cedar Cr.
Cannonball R.
Red R.
L. Oahe

SCALE/KEY

| 0 | 50 Miles |
| 0 | 50 Kilometers |

NP	National Park
NHS	National Historical Site
▲	Highest Point
▓	Mountains

lake in the state and has no outlet. Its water is slightly salty.

Lake Sakakawea is one of the world's largest artificially created lakes and North Dakota's largest body of water. It was created when the Garrison Dam contained the waters of the Missouri River near Riverdale. The lake has 1,600 miles (2,575 km) of shoreline. It is a popular spot for many forms of recreation, including fishing and boating.

The two biggest rivers in North Dakota are the Missouri and Red Rivers. The Missouri River drains about 60 percent of North Dakota, and the Red River drains most of the rest. North Dakota's lakes and rivers support a wide variety of fish, including bass, carp, catfish, northern pike, perch, sunfish, trout, and walleye.

Prairie Plants

Thanks to abundant summer sunlight, wild grasses grow to amazing heights in eastern North Dakota. Pioneers could get lost in a sea of grass well over their heads! Grasses in the western part of the state tend to be shorter and browner.

North Dakota's wild plants include beardtongue, black-eyed Susans, bluegrass, buffalo grass, chokeberry, gama grass, prairie mallow, red lily, and the state's flower, the wild prairie rose. North Dakota's trees include ash, aspen, basswood, box elder, elm, oak, poplar, and willow. Juniper trees and prickly pear cactus grow in the Badlands, along with many colorful spring flowers.

Birds and Beasts

Many birds thrive in North Dakota's abundant grasslands and lakes. Blackbirds, crows, eagles, larks, magpies, orioles, quail, robins, seagulls, sparrows, vultures, wild turkeys, western meadowlarks, and wrens are just a few of North Dakota's winged inhabitants.

Antelope, badgers, beavers, bobcats, coyotes, deer, lynx, mink, rabbit, raccoon, red foxes, skunks, squirrels, and weasels live in North Dakota. Prairie dogs build huge "dog towns" of elaborate underground burrows in the Badlands.

Bullsnakes and rattlers are among North Dakota's reptile residents.

▼ Prairie dogs live in underground communities or "towns" that include small social units called coteries. Each coterie usually contains one male, three or more females, and numerous young. Prairie dogs are very social creatures.

From Field to Factory

> When tillage begins, other arts follow. The farmers therefore are the founders of human civilization.
>
> — "Remarks on Agriculture" *Daniel Webster, January 13, 1840*

Cropland and pastures cover about 90 percent of North Dakota's total area. Agriculture accounts for a larger portion of North Dakota's gross product than it does in most states. Wheat is grown in every county and brings in more income than any other farm product in the state. Only Kansas grows more wheat. North Dakota leads the nation in both spring wheat and durum wheat, the kind used to make pasta. It is also a top producer of sunflower seeds, flaxseed (used to make linen and linseed oil, a key ingredient in paint), canola seeds, barley, oats, dry edible beans, soybeans, potatoes, rye, sugar beets, honey, and hay.

Agriculture and Beyond

Many of North Dakota's other important sources of income relate to its agricultural base, such as manufacturing farm equipment and processing and packing food. North Dakota's major food products include bread and pasta, frozen potato products (like French fries), and cooking oils made from oil seeds (like sunflower seeds). Dairy products include milk and cheddar cheese. The major meat products are steaks and sausages.

North Dakota also has a thriving livestock industry. Beef cattle are raised in the central and western plains and dairy cattle in the south-central part of the state. The cattle thrive on North Dakota's huge hay fields. Nearly one million calves are born in the state each year. Hogs are raised in the southeast and south-central parts of the state, where corn is plentiful. North Dakota farmers also raise sheep, chickens, and turkeys.

Other products made in North Dakota are construction

Top Employers
(of workers age sixteen and over)
Services 43.3%
Wholesale and retail trade 16.4%
Manufacturing . . 7.1%
Transportation, communications, and public utilities . . .8.0%
Construction 6.2%
Finance, insurance, and real estate . .5.9%
Federal, state, and local government (including military) 4.8%
Agriculture, forestry, fisheries, and mining 8.2%
Other 15.5%

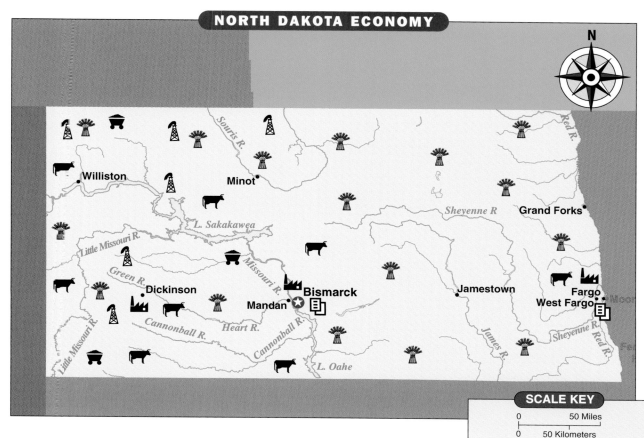

SCALE KEY

0	50 Miles
0	50 Kilometers

Cattle/Dairy
Farming
Manufacturing
Mining
Oil/Natural Gases
Services

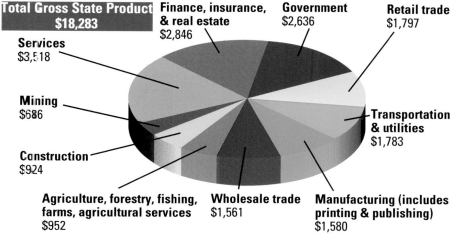

North Dakota Gross State Product — Millions of dollars

Total Gross State Product $18,283

- Finance, insurance, & real estate $2,846
- Government $2,636
- Retail trade $1,797
- Services $3,518
- Transportation & utilities $1,783
- Mining $686
- Construction $924
- Agriculture, forestry, fishing, farms, agricultural services $952
- Wholesale trade $1,561
- Manufacturing (includes printing & publishing) $1,580

and nonelectrical machinery, aircraft parts and other transportation equipment, computer disks and software, wood products (like cabinets and furniture), and stone, clay, and glass products. Newspapers are the leading type of printed material produced in the state.

Rich Resources

Soil may be North Dakota's greatest resource, but the state also has abundant minerals. The western part of North Dakota contains lignite coal beds (lignite is a soft, brown form of coal) that supply two-thirds of the lignite coal to the entire nation. These coal beds form one of the largest concentrations of solid fuel in the world.

Steam plants that burn lignite coal generate more than 90 percent of North Dakota's electric power. The Garrison Dam hydroelectric plant meets most of the rest of the state's energy needs. North Dakota produces enough power to export electricity by high-voltage transmission lines to other Midwestern states, chiefly Minnesota and Nebraska.

Petroleum, discovered in North Dakota in 1951, is the most valuable mineral in the state. It is produced mostly in wells in western North Dakota, where there are also wells that produce natural gas. Other useful minerals found in the state are sand, gravel, clay, sulfur, potash, gemstones, and salt.

Services and the Future

Most people in North Dakota today work in the service industries, including health care, real estate, business, legal, and personal services, finance, government, wholesale and retail trade, transportation, communication, and utilities. Service industry employees work in banks,

▲ North Dakota grows more sunflowers than any other state.

Wonderful Wheat

Wheat is one of ten thousand plant species classified as grasses, which include the most common food grains. Wheat flowers are small and not very showy, because they do not need to attract bees or birds. Like many other flowering plants, wheat is pollinated by the wind, which is in plentiful supply in North Dakota. Loose pollen on the male anthers floats on the breeze to the feathery female stigmas of neighboring wheat plants. Wheat, which feeds people and animals all over the world, was probably first cultivated nearly nine thousand years ago. The two largest wheat-producing countries are China and the United States. Wheat is also a major crop in Russia, India, Europe, Canada, Turkey, and Australia.

hospitals, military bases, offices, schools, and stores.

North Dakota is trying to broaden its economy, which still depends heavily on agriculture. The threat of crop failure and drops in farm prices haunts North Dakotans, who hope that increased industrial development will give the state greater economic security. Attracting new industry to North Dakota is difficult, however, because of its remote location. New industries that rely on telephones and the Internet may help North Dakota achieve its economic goals in the future.

▲ The Iverson No. 1 well, shown in this 1952 photograph, started North Dakota's oil boom when oil was discovered on this site in 1951.

Transportation and Communication

Transportation is vital to North Dakota, since it is a large state located far from the nation's key population centers. The state started to grow only when the railroads reached Fargo and Bismarck. Today, two rail lines provide freight service for North Dakota, and passenger lines serve several of the state's larger cities.

North Dakota has about 87,000 miles (140,013 km) of roads and highways. Interstate 94 travels east and west, passing near Fargo, Jamestown, and Bismarck. Interstate 29 runs north and south, along the state's eastern border. Several airlines serve North Dakota. The state's busiest commercial airport is in Fargo.

Made in North Dakota

Leading farm products and crops
Spring and durum wheat
Barley
Flaxseed
Oats
Honey
Sunflowers
Livestock

Other Products
Processed foods
Farm equipment
Energy

Major Airports		
Airport	Location	Passengers per year (2000)
Hector International Airport	Fargo	465,598
Bismark Municipal Airport	Bismark	268,879
Grand Forks Airport	Grand Forks	175,106

Serene and Strong

God of freedom, all victorious,
give us souls serene and strong,

Strength to make the future glorious,
keep the echo of our song.

North Dakota, North Dakota,
in our hearts forever long.

North Dakota, North Dakota,
in our hearts forever long.

"North Dakota Hymn,"
written in 1926 by James W. Foley;
music arranged by Dr. C. S. Putnam,
based on "The Austrian Hymn"

The Omnibus Bill of February 22, 1889, divided the Dakotas and allowed each state to create its own constitution. On July 4, 1889, North Dakota opened its constitutional convention. On October 1, the state constitution was voted upon and passed by the people. North Dakota's constitution divides the state government into three branches (the executive, the legislative, and the judicial), as modeled by the federal government. On November 2, 1889, President Benjamin Harrison admitted North (and South) Dakota into the Union.

The Executive Branch

North Dakota's governor leads the executive branch. The governor appoints important officials, submits a budget to the state legislature, and enforces North Dakota's laws. The governor is commander in chief of the state's military forces. He or she also has the power to sign bills into law, to veto (reject) bills, and to grant pardons.

Other members of the executive branch include the lieutenant governor, the attorney general, the secretary of state, the treasurer, the auditor, the superintendent of public instruction, and the commissioners of agriculture, insurance, and taxation.

State Constitution

"**W**e, the people of North Dakota, grateful to Almighty God for the blessings of civil and religious liberty, do ordain and establish this constitution."

— *Preamble to the 1889 North Dakota State Constitution*

Elected Posts in the Executive Branch		
Office	Length of Term	Term Limits
Governor	4 years	none
Lieutenant Governor	4 years	none
Secretary of State	4 years	none
Commissioner of Insurance	4 years	none
Attorney General	4 years	none
Superintendent of Public Instruction	4 years	none
State Superintendent	4 years	none
Commissioner of Agriculture	4 years	none
State Auditor	4 years	none
Tax Commissioner	4 years	none
Treasurer	4 years	none
Public Service Commissioner	6 years	none

The Legislative Branch

The legislative branch of the government creates new laws and oversees changes to existing laws. This branch consists of the forty-seven-member senate and the ninety-four-member house of representatives. Citizens in each of North Dakota's forty-seven districts elect one senator and two representatives to fill these posts.

A proposed new law is called a bill. A bill is voted on by the house and senate. If it passes, it goes to the governor, who passes or vetoes it. The house and senate vote again on a vetoed bill. If it passes by a two-thirds vote, it still becomes law.

The Judicial Branch

The judicial branch consists of district courts and the state supreme court. The supreme court rules on whether laws violate the state's constitution and handles appeals from district courts. If citizens think a trial is unfair, the case can be reviewed by the five justices of the state supreme court.

▼ The nineteen-story capitol in Bismarck is one of only four skyscraper capitols in the United States.

Party Politics

Through most of its history, North Dakota has favored the Republican party. North Dakotans have voted for Republican candidates in about four out of five presidential elections. In 1889, North Dakotans chose a Republican for their first governor. Republicans held that office for most of the next seventy years.

The state has a tradition of independent politics, however, especially in times of agricultural distress. In 1915, A. C. Townley, a socialist, organized the Nonpartisan League to help farmers who were seeking low-cost bank loans, grain storage, and processing facilities. By banding together, these farmers gained strength against greedy, out-of-state bankers and the powerful railroads. Within a year, the Nonpartisan League controlled North Dakota's government, founding a state-owned bank, mill, and grain elevator still controlled by the state today.

When the Nonpartisan League dissolved in 1956, many of its supporters joined the Democratic party. Since 1961, more Democrats have been elected governor than Republicans.

Controversial Figure

William L. Langer (1886–1959) was elected governor of North Dakota in 1932. A member of the Nonpartisan League, Langer took bold steps to help North Dakota's desperate farmers during the Great Depression. He was a decisive and outspoken person.

Then in 1934, Langer was convicted of cheating to win his election. He was removed from office. This decision was overturned in 1936. In 1938, Langer lost the governorship to a Democrat, but he was elected to the U.S. Senate in 1940 on the Republican ticket. Langer was reelected to the Senate three times, the last time as an independent. Langer died in 1959 while still serving in the U.S. Senate.

Legislative Assembly			
House	**Number of Members**	**Length of Term**	**Term Limits**
Senate	47 senators	4 years	No limit
House of Representatives	94 representatives	4 years	No limit

THEODORE ROOSEVELT (1901–1909)

So far, no president has hailed from North Dakota. But one credits the state with shaping him into a man who could become president. When Theodore Roosevelt went west in 1883, he was a skinny, frail, twenty-five-year-old with big, round glasses and a degree from Harvard His guide feared that Roosevelt would not be able to keep up on the strenuous hunting trip. But after the first day's 45-mile (72-km) horseback ride through rushing streams, timbered hills, and quicksand, Roosevelt was eager for more! By the end of the week, the young New Yorker had decided to buy a ranch in the rugged Badlands.

Roosevelt lived the life of a cowboy for two years. His thin frame filled out, and he learned to stay in the saddle no matter how hard his horse bucked. To his great delight, he even earned the respect of real cowmen. Twenty years later, Roosevelt reflected that it was in the West that the "romance of my life began."

When he returned to New York, Roosevelt ran for mayor. Though he lost that election, the political career that would eventually take him to the White House had begun. During the Spanish-American War in 1898, Roosevelt helped organize and lead the brave volunteer cavalry troop known as the Rough Riders. His confidence both in and out of the saddle was greatly aided by his Badlands adventure.

Governing Public Land

Some 3 2 million acres (1.30 million ha) of North Dakota belong to its citizens, including the National Grasslands, State Wildlife Management Areas, Waterfowl Production Areas, and National Wildlife Refuges. A variety of federal and state agencies, such as the North Dakota Game and Fish Department, the U.S. Fish and Wildlife Service, the Bureau of Land Management, North Dakota Forest Service, State Land Department, and the U.S. Army Corps of Engineers, manage the state's public land. These agencies enforce laws designed to strike a balance between the enjoyment of citizens and tourists today, and preservation for the future. Much of North Dakota's public land is kept open for hunting, fishing, and viewing wildlife. The state requires that anyone born after December 31, 1961, pass a certified hunter education course before obtaining a hunting license. Certain forms of hunting and fishing that take place in North Dakota require specific licenses.

▼ **Governor William Langer at his desk at the state capitol in 1937.**

Inspired by Nature

> I have always wished I could have been the first man west . . . to see it unblemished, unchanged, in all its original beauty. I came too late for that, so I wrote a story about a man who did.
> — *Louis L'Amour, author*

Long before people were inspired and challenged by North Dakota's amazing land, dinosaurs roamed the state. The Dakota Dinosaur Museum in Dickinson displays skeletons of many gigantic prehistoric beasts.

Writing Rock, near Grenora, gives visitors a glimpse into the life of the state's ancient Native Americans. This huge glacial boulder is covered with pictographs (picture writing). You can learn how later Native Americans coped with North Dakota's rugged climate by visiting the Knife River Indian Villages National Historical Site. In a reconstructed earth lodge, you can see backrests, pottery, baskets, and other items that would have been in a typical Hidatsa dwelling. Indentations on the ground along the nearby river show where hundreds of such lodges once stood. In their day, these villages had a total population of three thousand to five thousand.

You can celebrate the animal who sustained most of North Dakota's Natives at the National Buffalo Museum in Jamestown. Outside is an amazing 46-foot-long (14-m) concrete and steel statue of a buffalo. Also, the museum's herd includes White Cloud, a rare, albino (white) buffalo. To many Native Americans, a white buffalo is a sacred symbol of peace and hope. Inside the museum, you can see buffalo robes and buffalo-bone tools.

DID YOU KNOW?

The *Bismarck Tribune* published the first story describing the famous 1876 battle at Little Bighorn. The *Tribune*'s story was based on notes found in the buckskin pouch of a reporter killed in the battle.

▼ The giant buffalo statue at the National Buffalo Museum is the largest of its kind in the world.

Big Bison

Buffalo, or North American bison, are wild, humpbacked, shaggy-haired oxen. A male bison can weigh more than 2,000 pounds (907 kg) and stand 6 feet (1.8 m) tall at the shoulder. Females average 930 pounds (422 kg) and stand 5 feet (1.5 m) tall. The matted fur on a buffalo's forehead is so thick it has been known to stop a bullet! Buffalo calves grow in their mother's womb for about nine months, the same as human babies.

Once bison ranged over almost the entire North American continent in the millions. They provided meat, milk, shelter, shoes, clothing, and tools for Plains Indians. Buffalo chips (dried buffalo dung) were used for fuel where wood was scarce. Herds of buffalo are making a comeback in protected areas of North Dakota. The bison grazing in the photo above are part of a herd of more than five hundred buffalo that roam through Theodore Roosevelt National Park in the northwestern part of the state.

The Turtle Mountain Chippewa Heritage Center has historical and cultural displays of the Ojibwa (also known as Chippewa) people, who also rose to the challenge of life in North Dakota.

The Lewis and Clark Interpretive Center in Washburn gives guests a chance to learn about the famous Expedition. Exhibits range from what the explorers wore to the music they played and the canoes they paddled. You can even strap on a cradleboard like the one Sacagawea used to carry her infant son, Jean-Baptiste, on the westward trek.

The nearby reconstruction of Fort Mandan lets visitors walk through simple log buildings, like those that sheltered Lewis and Clark during the first winter of their journey. The fort was built several miles from three Hidatsa and two Mandan villages, in order to avoid seeming to favor one village over another.

The struggles of North Dakota's settlers are recalled at Bonanzaville, USA, in West Fargo. This preserved pioneer village features forty buildings, including a church, one-room schoolhouse, general store, log cabin, town hall, jail, drugstore, hotel, and Fargo's first house, built in 1869. In August, Pioneer Days give visitors a peek into the crafts and skills of the past. The North Dakota Heritage Center, near Lake Sakakawea, also has exhibits relating to frontier

life, from tools to toys to letters full of hope and desperation written to the families the settlers left behind. The town of Medora offers another chance to see early North Dakota, including the lavish house built by the Marquis de Mores, who founded the town in 1883.

North Dakota's eighteen state parks and campgrounds include many historic and military sites. At Fort Abraham Lincoln State Park, you can stand on the site from which George Armstrong Custer set out on the ill-fated expedition to the Battle of Little Bighorn. Parts of the fort, including Custer's home, have been reconstructed.

Fort Stevenson State Park was named for a late 1800s frontier fort that served as a supply depot for military posts. Today, the site offers visitors a chance to enjoy North Dakota's excellent fishing. It is close to the North Dakota Fishing Hall of Fame.

Theodore Roosevelt National Park honors the memory of the president who drove cattle and hunted in the Badlands in the 1880s. Roosevelt's experience of the natural beauty of North Dakota inspired him to advance the cause of conservation once he was elected. During his presidency, he

▲ Portrait of Mandan-Hidatsa Indian woman taken at Fort Abraham Lincoln State Park.

DID YOU KNOW?

North Dakotans have invented a new sport! As part of a Fourth of July contest in the 1970s, some North Dakotans held a lawnmower race. Since then, folks have been fixing up their mowers to race up to sixty miles per hour (97 km/h) instead of the usual speed of five (8 km/h). Racing circuits have sprung up across the state, and news-papers report the action.

founded the U.S. Forest Service, signed the National Monuments Act, and established the first federal game preserve. His conservation efforts led to the founding of the National Park Service, which protects unspoiled places, such as his beloved North Dakota Badlands.

Schools and Libraries

North Dakota's students score high on achievement tests and have the lowest dropout rate in the nation. The school system has two problems, however. Because many of North Dakota's small towns are shrinking, some graduating classes contain only two students per year. North Dakotans are not sure whether or not small-town schools should merge to create bigger schools with better facilities, because two negative results would be long bus rides through bad weather and a higher student-to-teacher ratio. Along with scattered students, the state's schools also face trouble attracting and keeping good teachers. Because North Dakota teacher salaries are low, many teachers take jobs out of state.

In 1883, the University of North Dakota became the state's first institution of higher education. The state currently has six four-year state universities. The largest are the Univerisity of North Dakota at Grand Forks, with

▼ Theodore Roosevelt's Maltese Cross Ranch Cabin, originally located near Medora, is now part of Theodore Roosevelt National Park.

branches in Williston and Devils Lake, and North Dakota State Univerity at Fargo, with a branch at Bottineau. The state also has several junior colleges and a few private colleges.

Women's clubs did much for North Dakota's early libraries. In 1897, a woman's club opened the state's first public library at Grafton. In 1898, the state Department of Public Instruction set up traveling libraries to serve the schools. Today, North Dakota has numerous public libraries.

The Arts

North Dakota offers various opportunities for entertainment and the arts. Fargo, Grand Forks, and Minot have symphony orchestras that play concerts statewide. Each summer, the International Peace Garden, on the border between North Dakota and Canada, hosts an International Music Camp for gifted young musicians. Summer is also the season for numerous powwows, rodeos, and ethnic festivals throughout the state, as well as musicals at Fort Totten Indian Reservation, south of Devils Lake. The state has several other summer theaters. Year-round, visitors can enjoy the Plains Art Museum in Fargo, a large fine-arts museum specializing in Native American art and works by Plains painters.

Outdoor Fun

North Dakotans enjoy a variety of outdoor activities, such as berry picking, bird watching, bike riding, hiking, and horseback riding. Every warm weekend, Lake Sakakawea and many of the state's smaller lakes and rivers fill with people boating and fishing. The state has many golf courses and seventeen speedways for car racing.

North Dakotans do not let a little ice interfere with their fun. Citizens pride themselves on finding ways to enjoy the cold. Some residents water their yards to create ice rinks; others just skate on the frozen streets, ponds, and lakes. The popularity of ice skating in North

▲ Aerial view of Peace Park located on the North Dakota and Saskatchewan, Canada border.

Dakota relates not only to the climate, but to the heritage of many of the state's residents who came from Scandinavia. Ice skating was probably invented in the Scandinavian countries before the birth of Christ. The first skates are believed to have been sharp splinters of animal bone attached to the bottom of boots to make traveling over ice easier. The modern word "skate" comes from the Dutch word *schaats*, which means "leg bone." In the thirteenth and fourteenth centuries, wood replaced the bone in skate blades. Iron eventually replaced the wood. But since iron dulls quickly, steel became the blade of choice.

Snowmobiling, skiing, and ice fishing are all popular activities in the state. Each January, twenty-five hundred people cut holes in frozen Devils Lake to see who can catch the biggest fish. The minute temperatures rise above freezing, hearty North Dakotans get spring fever, taking off hats and gloves to revel in the relative warmth.

Mighty Maris

Long-time North Dakota resident Roger Maris (born in 1934) was offered a football scholarship but chose to play professional baseball for the Cleveland Indians. In 1960, Maris hit thirty-nine home runs for the Yankees, winning the Most Valuable Player (MVP) Award. In 1961, Maris neared Babe Ruth's thirty-four-year-old record of sixty homers in one season. As Maris neared the record, he stayed cool, despite the tremendous pressure. Maris hit homer number sixty-one on the last day of the season. He went on to win the MVP Award a second time and to lead his teams to the World Series seven times. His record for most home runs in a single season stood for thirty-seven years. Maris died of lymphatic cancer in 1985 at the age of fifty-one.

▼ Roger Maris slugs a home run during the 1961 baseball season on his way to breaking Babe Ruth's record.

The Cream of the Crop

If it had not been for what I learned during those years that I spent here in North Dakota, I would never have been president of the United States."

— *Theodore Roosevelt, Fargo, 1910, reflecting on the resilience and resourcefulness of the people of the state where he lived the life of a cowboy*

Following are only a few of the thousands of people who were born, died, or spent much of their lives in North Dakota and made extraordinary contributions to the state and the nation.

SACAGAWEA
EXPLORER AND GUIDE
BORN: *c. 1786, near Salmon, Idaho*
DIED: *1812 or 1884 (exact date unknown)*

This young Shoshone woman acted as guide and interpreter for Lewis and Clark, explorers sent by President Thomas Jefferson to blaze a water route to the Pacific Ocean through the new territory. Sacagawea, with her husband and infant son, joined the Expedition at Fort Mandan, near modern-day Bismarck. During the tough wilderness trek, she showed them which plants were safe to eat and helped them pass safely through tribal territories. Sacagawea persuaded the Shoshone to help the Expedition and was reunited with her brother, Shoshone Chief Cameahwait, during that time.

Sacagawea traveled to the Pacific Ocean with the Expedition. After that, her story is uncertain. According to one account, she died in 1812, along the Missouri River. According to another, Sacagawea lived on the Shoshone reservation until she reached the age of a hundred. Sacagawea is one of the most-honored women in American history. A mountain, a river, and a pass are just a few of the memorials to Sacagawea scattered along the route of her amazing journey.

CARL BEN EIELSON
PIONEERING AVIATOR
BORN: *July 20, 1897, Hatton, ND*
DIED: *November 9, 1929, off the coast of Alaska*

Carl Ben Eielson learned to fly during World War I, then took a teaching job in Alaska. Soon he was flying mail, supplies, and passengers. In 1926, explorer Hubert Wilkins hired Eielson to fly over the North Pole. They were stopped by a blizzard, but Eielson became the first pilot to fly over the Arctic Ocean. In 1927, engine trouble prevented the pole crossing, but Eielson became the first person to land a plane on floating ice. In an amazing feat of Arctic survival, the two walked 12 days, 125 miles (201 km), to the nearest settlement. In 1928, they flew over the North Pole to Norway! Eielson flew out in a blizzard in 1929 to rescue passengers on a ship stuck in the ice off the coast of Alaska. He never returned. A mountain and an air force base in Alaska were named after Eielson.

LAWRENCE WELK
ORCHESTRA LEADER
BORN: *March 11, 1903, Strasburg, ND*
DIED: *May 17, 1992, Santa Monica, CA*

Lawrence Welk grew up in a sod house near Strasburg, the sixth of nine children. Strasburg was a small, German-speaking community. Welk did not learn English until he was twenty-one. He earned his first accordion by hiring himself out as a farm laborer. He broke into show business by playing accordion for local dances. Radio, and later television, brought him to a national audience. Welk hosted television's most popular "golden oldies" program for twenty-seven years, from 1955 to 1982. His "champagne orchestra" was adored by millions.

ERA BELL THOMPSON
JOURNALIST
BORN: *August 10, 1905, Des Moines, IA*
DIED: *December 30, 1986, Chicago, IL*

Although she was born in Iowa, Era Bell's family moved to a Driscoll farm when she was five. While attending the University of North Dakota, Era established five state women's track records and tied two national intercollegiate women's track records. Thompson worked her way up in journalism, making a reputation by reporting on black issues in the United States and around the world. In 1964, she became the international editor of *Ebony* magazine. Thompson's autobiography, *American Daughter*, describes her childhood in North Dakota. She also wrote *Africa, Land of My Father* and *White On Black*.

CASPER OIMOEN
CHAMPION SKIER
BORN: *May 6, 1906, Valdres, Norway*
DIED: *July 27, 1995, Ashland, OR*

Casper Oimoen learned to ski when he was a boy in Norway. He started on barrel staves — the curved planks used to make barrels — instead of real skis. In 1923, Oimoen's family moved to

Minot, and seventeen-year-old Casper began winning ski jumping contests. He could not compete in the 1928 Olympics because he was not yet a U.S. citizen. But he continued to win an amazing number of skiing medals and trophies — a total of four hundred in his career. During the 1930s, Oimoen worked as a bricklayer, a trade he learned from his uncle in Minot. He was part of the construction crew that built North Dakota's state capitol in Bismarck. In 1936, Oimoen was captain of the U.S. Olympic Ski Team. In 1963, he was inducted into the U.S. Skiing Hall of Fame. The bronze statue of Oimoen in a Minot park shows him standing tall with a pair of skis.

Louis L'Amour
BESTSELLING AUTHOR
BORN: *March 22, 1908, Jamestown, ND*
DIED: *June 10, 1988, Los Angeles, CA*

Louis L'Amour's father was a farm-machinery salesman and Jamestown's Chief of Police. An avid reader, young L'Amour yearned for adventure. At fifteen, he left home to see the country and found work as a miner, hay baler, lumberjack, circus roustabout, and prizefighter. Listening to people's stories, L'Amour fell in love with the rugged individuals who had settled the West. In the 1950s, he started writing Western novels. L'Amour published more than 400 short stories and more than 100 novels. He wrote 65 television scripts, and sold more than 30 scripts to the movie industry, including *Hondo,* which starred John Wayne. L'Amour's books have sold in excess of 200 million copies, and are still popular. He ranks among the most beloved U.S. writers.

Eric Sevareid
JOURNALIST
BORN: *November 26, 1912, Velva, ND*
DIED: *July 9, 1992, Washington, D.C.*

While he was growing up in Velva, Sevareid was fascinated by the local newspaper. He knew at an early age that he wanted to become a journalist. At eighteen, Sevareid started working as a copy boy. While attending the University of Minnesota, he became a reporter for the *Minneapolis Journal*. After receiving his B.A., Sevareid went to London and Paris to continue his studies. He joined the Paris edition of the *New York Herald*. In 1939, he became a radio correspondent for CBS. He achieved fame for his radio reports from the European battlefields of World War II. After the war, Sevareid entered the new world of television, eventually becoming the commentator on the *CBS Evening News*. He was known for his coverage of presidential elections and meetings of the United Nations Assembly in Paris. By the time he retired in 1977, Eric Sevareid was one of the nation's most respected radio and television journalists.

Peggy Lee
SINGER AND SONGWRITER
BORN: *May 26,1920, Jamestown, ND*
DIED: *January 22, 2002, Bel Air, CA*

Born Norma Dolores Egstrom, Peggy Lee grew up singing in church choirs in Jamestown. After high school, Lee went to Hollywood to become a star and wound up as a waitress. Lee returned to North Dakota where a Fargo radio station hired her as a singer. In 1941, popular swing band leader Benny Goodman discovered the stylish singer. Then Lee wrote many of her biggest hit songs. She provided the voices for Peg the dog and both Siamese cats in Disney's animated film *Lady and the Tramp*. She wrote six of the film's popular songs, including "We Are Siamese."

WARREN CHRISTOPHER
POLITICIAN

BORN: *October 27, 1925, Scranton, ND*

Warren Christopher became the deputy secretary of state under President Jimmy Carter and then secretary of state under President Bill Clinton. During Carter's administration, Christopher helped negotiate the return of fifty-two Americans taken hostage at the U.S. Embassy in Iran. For this achievement, he was awarded the Medal of Freedom in 1981.

ANGIE DICKINSON (BORN ANGELINE BROWN)
ACTRESS

BORN: *September 30, 1931, Kulm, ND*

Angeline Brown was born in Kulm, where her family owned the weekly newspaper. The Browns moved to California when Angie was ten. While working as a secretary, Angie entered beauty contests and was spotted by a talent scout. Angie acquired her professional name when she married college football star Gene Dickinson. Her breakthrough role came at age twenty-seven, when she played opposite John Wayne in Howard Hawks' 1959 classic Western, *Rio Bravo*. In 1960, Dickinson played Frank Sinatra's wife in *Ocean's Eleven*. She had a small part in the 2001 remake, which featured Julia Roberts in Dickinson's role. Throughout the 1960s, Dickinson was a major movie star in mostly minor films. In 1964, she starred with Ronald Reagan in his last feature film, *The Killers*. From 1966–1980, Dickinson was married to the popular composer Burt Bacharach. Angie Dickinson is best known for playing a tough, smart detective in the 1970s TV series *Police Woman*, but she has appeared in more than fifty film and TV productions.

PHYLLIS FRELICH
ACTRESS

BORN: *February 29, 1944, near Devils Lake*

Phyllis Frelich was the oldest of nine deaf children born to deaf parents. She grew up on a farm near Devils Lake. After attending the School for the Deaf in Devils Lake, Frelich devoured the few theater courses offered by Gallaudet College, a liberal arts school for the deaf in Washington, D.C. In the 1960s, Frelich helped found the National Theater for the Deaf (NTD). Through the NTD, she met playwright Mark Medoff. Frelich inspired him to write *Children of a Lesser God*, a play concerning the problems of being deaf in a hearing world. Frelich's excellent performance in Medoff's play on Broadway in 1981 won her a Tony Award. Recently, Frelich has made guest appearances on TV in *E.R.* and *Diagnosis Murder*. She also starred in the Hallmark Hall of Fame made-for-television movie *Love is Never Silent*.

North Dakota

History At-A-Glance

10,000 B.C.
Giant bison, mammoths, and mastodons roam lush forest of what will one day become North Dakota. Paleo-Indians hunt the giant beasts.

A.D. 1000
Mandans establish villages along the Missouri River; they are soon joined by Arikaras and Hidatsas and later Ojibwa and Sioux.

1682
France claims lands drained by Missouri River, including most of North Dakota.

1738
French explorer Pierre Gaultier de Varennes de la Vérendrye becomes the first known European to enter North Dakota.

1803
U.S. gains the southwestern part of North Dakota from France in Louisiana Purchase.

1818
U.S. gains northeastern North Dakota from Great Britain; North Dakota becomes part of Missouri Territory.

1857
Fort Abercrombie, North Dakota's first military post, is built in Southern Red River Valley to protect supply lines and help pioneers.

1861
Congress creates Dakota Territory.

1862
U.S. government signs treaties with Sioux granting them land on reservations.

1863
The Dakota Territory is opened to homesteading.

1860s–70s
Indian Wars — Federal troops suppress Native American uprisings prompted by land grabs and broken treaties.

1872
Northern Pacific Railroad begins laying tracks in North Dakota.

1600   **1700**   **1800**

1492
Christopher Columbus comes to New World.

1607
Capt. John Smith and three ships land on Virginia coast and start first English settlement in New World — Jamestown.

1754–63
French and Indian War.

1773
Boston Tea Party.

1776
Declaration of Independence adopted July 4.

1777
Articles of Confederation adopted by Continental Congress.

1787
U.S. Constitution written.

1812–14
War of 1812.

United States

History At-A-Glance

1881
Sioux chief Sitting Bull surrenders to U.S. soldiers. Sioux and Ojibwa tribes give up most of eastern North Dakota to U.S. government.

1881
Northern Pacific Railroad completes a line across North Dakota. Professional hunters shoot buffalo from trains, nearly wiping out the herds.

1882
North Dakota's Native Americans are forced onto four reservations.

1890–1910
North Dakota's population more than doubles.

1912
North Dakota becomes first state to hold a national presidential primary.

1947
Construction begins on Garrison Dam to provide irrigation, flood control, and hydroelectric power.

1947
Theodore Roosevelt National Memorial Park is founded.

1951
Oil is discovered near Tioga.

1954
Garrison Dam is completed, forming Lake Sakakawea.

1966
Most severe blizzard in North Dakota's history.

1988
North Dakota is hit with first major drought since the 1930s.

1997
Severe flooding strikes Red River Valley.

1800   **1900**   **2000**

1848
Gold discovered in California draws eighty thousand prospectors in the 1849 Gold Rush.

1861–65
Civil War.

1869
Transcontinental railroad completed.

1917–18
U.S. involvement in World War I.

1929
Stock market crash ushers in Great Depression.

1941–45
U.S. involvement in World War II.

1950–53
U.S. fights in the Korean War.

1964–73
U.S. involvement in Vietnam War.

2000
George W. Bush wins the closest presidential election in history.

2001
A terrorist attack in which four hijacked airliners crash into New York City's World Trade Center, the Pentagon, and farmland in western Pennsylvania leaves thousands dead or injured.

◄ **In this circa 1850 engraving travelers meet with the Minatarre Indians near Fort Clark.**

Festivals and Fun for All

Check web site for exact date and directions.

The Big One Arts and Crafts, Minot

Minot offers two crafts festivals each year, during the first weekend in April and the first weekend in November. See all kinds of crafts, toys, games, and puzzles. www.thebigone.biz

Birding and Nature Festival, Devils Lake

In August, Sully's Hill National Game Preserve offers tours and workshops on birding-by-ear, bird identification, and butterflies. Look at critters close-up, ride in a hot-air balloon, kayak, or listen to a speech by an actor portraying a historical figure, such as Theodore Roosevelt. www.sullyshillbirdfest.com

Dakota Heritagefest, Jamestown

Come to the Jamestown Civic Center to see entertainment like the Polish National Alliance Dancers, the Dakota Key Accordion Band, and Jamestown's own Choralaires male choral group. www.dakotaheritagefest.com

Fargo Film Festival, Fargo

Since 2000, downtown's beautifully restored, Art Deco, 870-seat Historic Fargo Theatre offers screenings of independent and student films, presentations, and panel discussions starting on Wednesday evening of the first full week in March. www.fargotheatre.com

Fort Union Rendezvous, near Williston

Williston's largest event takes place during the third full weekend in June, with people in period costumes living in canvas teepees or tents, selling and demonstrating crafts such as woodworking, flint carving, fire-starting, and skinning. Bagpipers and fiddlers play period music. www.nps.gov/fous

Living History Field Day, Fort Totten State Historic Site, near Devils Lake

In early September, the buildings on this historic site come alive with demonstrations of skills such as bricklaying, tanning, teepee building, soap and candle making, and more. www.discovernd.com

Mandan Rodeo Days, Mandan

This is a citywide Fourth-of-July celebration that coincides with Mandan's art-in-the-park art show.
701-220-2959

Norsk Hostfest

This five-day celebration of Scandinavian heritage during the second week of October includes fun like crafts, a Scandinavian dessert contest, a play, and a rodeo.
www.hostfest.com

North Dakota State Fair, Minot

For nine days, starting on the third weekend in July, Minot hosts a good, old-fashioned state fair with a wide variety of exhibits; competitions for best livestock, cooking, needlework, plants, and flowers; carnival rides; concerts; and more.
www.ndstatefair.com

Planes on the Plains, Casselton

This air show, sponsored by North Dakota's chapter of the Experimental Aviation Association during the third weekend in July, features amazing planes doing amazing things and a chance for kids to attend ground school, and more.
www.casselton.com

Shiverfest, Devils Lake

Usually the second weekend in February, this annual fun fest includes sled-dog races, a kids' ice-fishing contest, snowmobile rides and races, ice golf, an evening cook-off, and music.
www.devilslakend.com

Northern Plains Indian Culture Fest, Stanton

Teepees and other exhibits and activities during the Northern Plains Indian Culture Fest in Stanton demonstrate how the Plains tribes lived for thousands of years before the arrival of European explorers.
www.nps.gov/knri/event.htm

Ukrainian Festival, Dickinson

Two-week workshops teach children and adults Ukrainian language, dance, and songs in preparation for performances during the third weekend in July. A Ukrainian buffet, artwork, Sunday masses, and a dance add to the celebration.
www.ukrainianculturalinstitute.com

White Cloud's Birthday/Tatanka Festival, Jamestown

All of Jamestown celebrates the birthday of the white buffalo that lives at the National Buffalo Museum. Enjoy free birthday cake and a party with Native American dancers, plus a kids carnival, parade, and speakers.
www.jamestownnd.com

▶ Norsk Hostfest, the annual Scandinavian festival that draws people from around the world, has added strong man competitions to its cultural attractions.

Books

Bohner, Charles. *Bold Journey: West with Lewis & Clark*. New York, NY: Houghton Mifflin, 1990. Learn more about the first American exploration of North Dakota and the other lands included in the Louisiana Purchase.

Hintz, Martin. *North Dakota*. (America the Beautiful: Second Series). Danbury, CT: Children's Press, 2000. See spectacular photos of North Dakota.

Pearson, Ethelyn. *It Really Happened Here: Amazing Tales of Minnesota and the Dakotas*. Gwinner, ND: McCleery & Sons, 2000. Learn surprising facts about North Dakota's history.

St. George, Judith. *Sacagawea*. New York, NY: Philomel Books, 1997. Learn more about the young Shoshone woman who guided Lewis and Clark on their journey.

Web Sites

▶ Official state web sites
www.state.nd.us
www.northdakota.com

▶ North Dakota Tourism
www.ndtourism.com
www.ndstatefair.com

▶ North Dakota Historical Society
www.state.nd.us/hist/sites.htm

▶ North Dakota's Library System
www.lib.ndsu.nodak.edu/reference/ndakota.html

▶ Fort Mandan/Lewis & Clark Interpretive Center
www.fortmandan.com

▶ Hiking and backpacking
www.northcountrytrail.org

▶ North Dakota's state parks
www.ndparks.com